Astronaut

written by

Karen Hoenecke

KAEDEN ❤ BOOKS™

Title: Astronaut
Copyright © 2013 Kaeden Corporation
Author: Karen Hoenecke
Design: Signature Design
PHOTOGRAPHY CREDITS
Cover Photos.com. **4, 5, 9** NASA.
6, KRT. **7, 8** Getty/NASA

ISBN-13: 978-1-61181-377-7

Published by:
     Kaeden Corporation
     P. O. Box 16190
     Rocky River, Ohio 44116
     1-(800)-890-READ(7323)
     www.kaeden.com

Printed in Guangzhou, China
NOR/0613/CA21301049

First edition 1997
Second Edition 2004
Third edition 2013

Table of Contents

Suiting Up

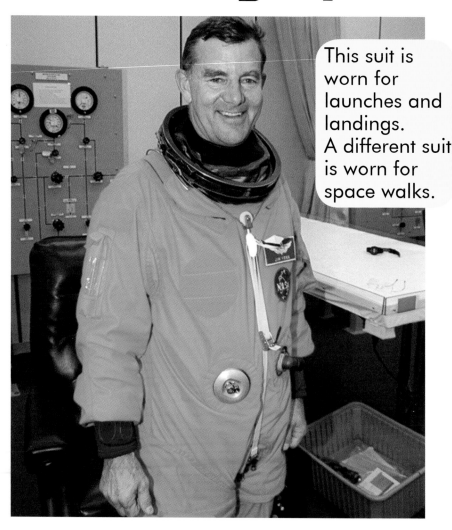

This suit is worn for launches and landings. A different suit is worn for space walks.

An **astronaut** puts on the suit.

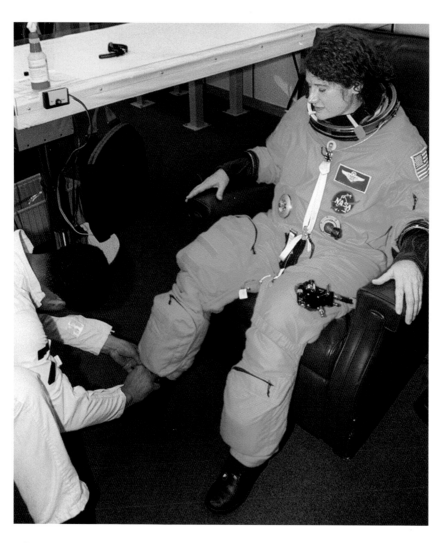

An astronaut puts on
the boots.

The helmet has a black sunshade to block out glare from the sun.

An astronaut puts on the **helmet**.

An astronaut puts on the gloves.

Ready for Blast Off

The astronauts wear orange suits so they are easy to find if they have to evacuate.

The astronauts are ready to go.

5...4...3...2...1

Blast off!

Glossary

astronaut - a person who is trained for space travel

helmet - a protective head covering

Index